GLENN WEISER

TIN PAN ALLEY
FAVORITES FOR
FINGERSTYLE GUITAR

FOREWORD BY CHIP DEFFAA

To access audio visit:
www.halleonard.com/mylibrary

Enter Code
1903-8718-6695-5159

ISBN 978-1-57424-395-6
SAN 683-8022

Cover by James Creative Group

Copyright © 2020 CENTERSTREAM Publishing
P.O. Box 17878 - Anaheim Hills, CA 92817

www.centerstream-usa.com | centerstrm@aol.com | 714-779-9390

CONTENTS

FOREWORD....

The gifted Glenn Weiser, who's given us 15 music books, plus more than 100 published articles on music, now offers us the first book of solo guitar arrangements of songs from the golden era of Tin Pan Alley. Whether you're a young player or a seasoned pro, you'll find much to savor here. And Weiser's engaging arrangements respect the composers' original intentions while working perfectly for contemporary ears. His wonderfully rich knowledge of roots music makes any new offering from him a treat.

The songs Weiser has chosen open windows onto the past. George M. Cohan's immortal "The Yankee Doodle Boy" and "You're a Grand Old Flag" capture the jaunty pride of an early 20th century America that was just beginning to find its place in the world. Cohan was honored with a Congressional gold medal for his "contributions to the American spirit." Two of Al Jolson's signature songs, "April Showers" and "California, Here I Come," recall the era when Jolson uniquely enjoyed the freedom to interpolate into his Broadway shows any songs he liked.

Here, too, is the number that made young Irving Berlin the most famous songwriter in the world, "Alexander's Ragtime Band." Berlin originally introduced this song as an instrumental–and it flopped! Then he added lyrics, premiering the song at a Friars Frolic benefit show–and the song became the most successful new number in decades.

You'll find in this collection the best-known and best-selling of all blues numbers, W. C. Handy's "St. Louis Blues." And Bessie Smith's immortal "Nobody Knows You When You're Down and Out." And the timeless "Lovesick Blues." In the 1920s, Emmett Miller made the best recording of that song. A generation later, Hank Williams, who was tremendously influenced by Miller, scored a huge success with his own terrific version.

You'll find here, too, "Pretty Baby," which started out as a song New Orleans singer/pianist Tony Jackson wrote for his boyfriend, and was revised by Gus Kahn and Egbert Van Alstyne to become a national favorite. And James P. Johnson and Cecil Mack's "Charleston," which helped define the whole Jazz Age. With composer Vincent Youmans, lyricist Irving Caesar created one of the most-recorded songs of all time, "Tea for Two." However, Caesar told me, the lyrics that Caesar created were originally intended by him to be simply "dummy lyrics"–place-holders, to help him remember the rhyme scheme. But Youmans liked those lyrics--and so did the public!

I like these songs. I like the way Weiser interprets them. These numbers are pure Americana. And this is a wonderful collection. I hope he will do a follow-up. I'll buy the first copy!

– CHIP DEFFAA
(Deffaa, who for many years reviewed music and theater for The New York Post, is the author of eight books and 18 plays.)

INTRODUCTION

In the first decades of the 20th century, a passerby walking on 28th St. in New York City between 5th and 6th Avenues during business hours in the summertime would have heard a cacophony of notes from upright pianos coming through the open windows of the dozens of music publishing houses clustered there. Amidst the din he might have picked out a tune destined to become a timeless standard of popular music, because these two blocks on either side of Broadway were where America's hits were born. The street, and the industry located there, became known as "Tin Pan Alley."

The nickname was coined by the press around 1900, as "tin pan" was slang for a decrepit old piano. Tin Pan Alley's importance lay in the fact that hits were not yet measured in records sold or radio play, but rather by sheet music sales. With many households having a piano or at least a ukulele the family could gather around to sing with, there was a steady demand for the catchy songs that the Alley supplied. New hits were also worked into running Broadway shows, boosting sales even more.

These songs became the soundtrack of the Jazz Age as well. As "sweet" dance bands like Paul Whiteman's in New York City played polished orchestral arrangements of standards, the "hot' black jazz ensembles in Chicago led by King Oliver, Jimmie Noone, Louis Armstrong and others advanced the art of ad-lib soloing from 12-bar blues and New Orleans tunes to improvising over the chords of the latest hits.

Plectrum guitarists of the 1920s such as Lonnie Johnson, Eddie Lang, and Django Reinhardt were the first to record Tin Pan Alley tunes with jazz bands. By the early 1930s, a small circle of guitar players in Muhlenberg County, Kentucky were working out solo fingerstyle versions of standards. Kennedy Jones taught alternate thumb picking to coal miners Mose Rager and Ike Everly (Ike was the father of the Everly Brothers), and the pair would roam the area playing for parties, dances, and other occasions. Like Jones, they featured a wide range of material which besides blues and folk music included Alley songs. A local teenager, Merle Travis, learned the 'Kentucky thumbpick' style created by Jones from the older players (Jones first began using a thumbpick because of a blister on his thumb, and the practice caught on). The style became widespread when Tennessean Chet Atkins, who listened to Travis' radio show and improved the technique by picking with three fingers instead of one, passed it on to a new generation of guitarists including Tommy Emmanuel, John Knowles, Tom Bresh, and Richard Smith.

When I began playing guitar in the mid-1960s I learned many Alley tunes from my mom, a pianist with a large sheet music collection. I would sit on the piano bench next to her and we would play "Charleston," April Showers," "The Birth of the Blues," "Pretty Baby," and other gems. By the 1970s, I began to work out many of them for fingerstyle guitar. Over the years I created dozens of arrangements of hits from the era, leading to the present volume.

This book is a collection of 31 classic songs from Tin Pan Alley's heyday, arranged for solo guitar with notation, tablature, fingering indications, chord symbols, and online audio. These standards celebrate things like landmark events, popular pastimes, nationalities, cities and states, patriotism, and love won and lost. I have arranged them from the original sheet music, with occasional melodic embellishments and chord substitutions. I hope you'll find them as much fun to play as I have.

If you'd like to study these arrangements with me, I offer private guitar lessons via Skype, Zoom, or FaceTime. For details, visit my website at www.celticguitarmusic.com.
Enjoy the music!

Glenn Weiser
Southwick, MA
May, 2020

After You've Gone

This gorgeous torch song was first recorded in 1918 by Marion Harris
and has been covered by famous artists in every decade since then.

Turner Layton
Henry Creamer, 1918

Arr. G. Weiser

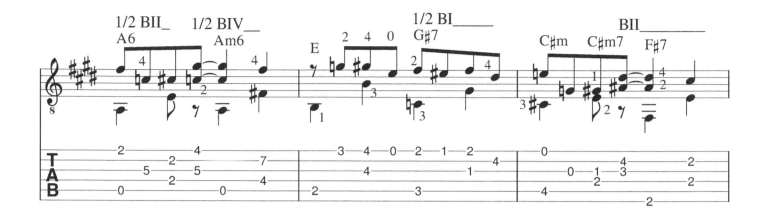

7

Ain't We Got Fun

Gus Kahn
Raymond B. Egan
Richard A. Whiting, 1920

This famous foxtrot debuted in the revue *Satires of 1920*. The lyrics describe a couple unfazed by their poverty.

Arr. G. Weiser

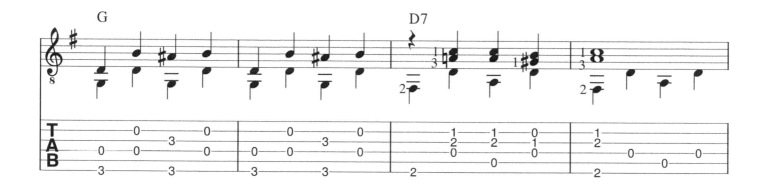

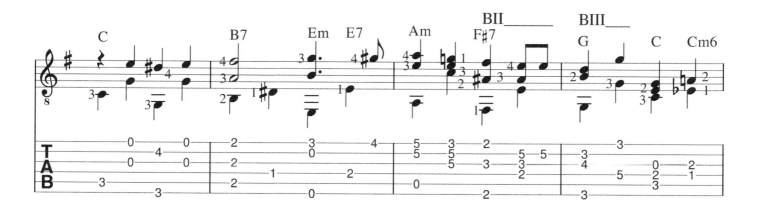

9

Alabama Jubilee

This popular song became a country music standard, and has been recorded
by The Skillet Lickers, Red Foley, and The Kentucky Colonels.

Geo. L Cobb
Jack Yellen, 1915

Arr. G. Weiser

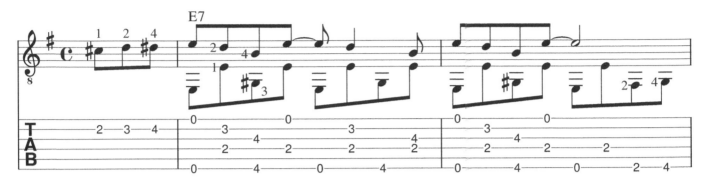

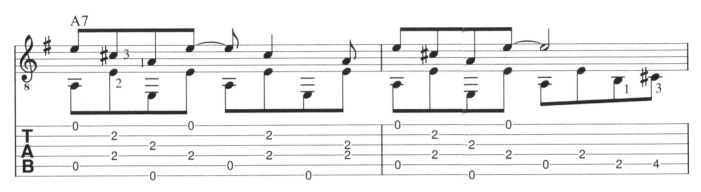

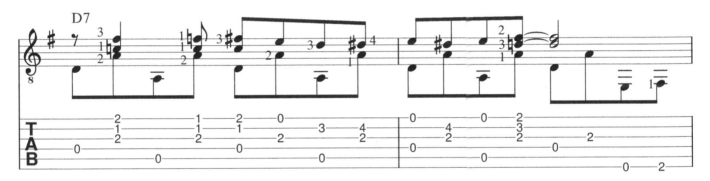

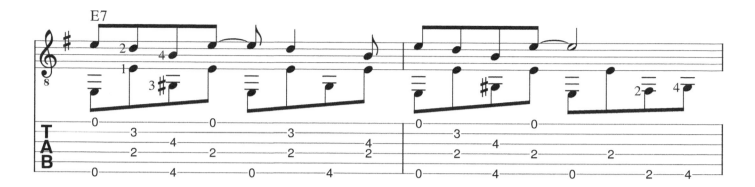

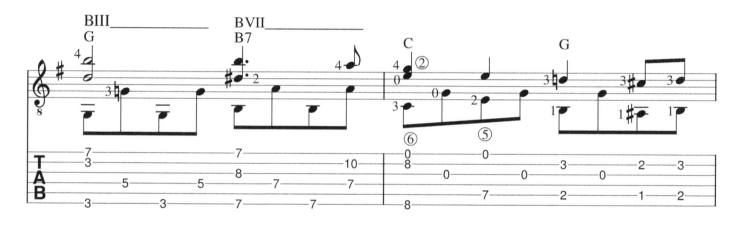

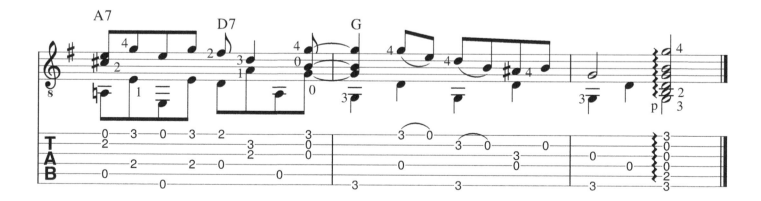

11

Alexander's Ragtime Band

This was the first major hit by Irving Berlin, one of America's most prolific and
successful songwriters. The lyrics are thought to refer to the jazz orchestra
of Alexander Watzke, a popular white band leader in New Orleans.

Irving Berlin, 1911

Arr. G. Weiser

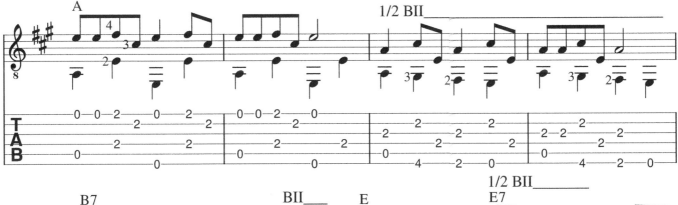

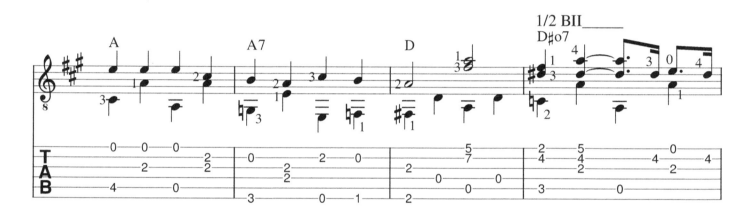

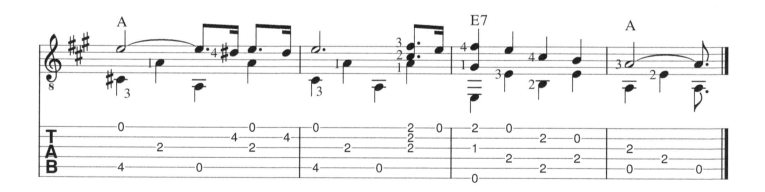

13

April Showers

This is from the 1921 musical *Bombo*, starring Al Jolson. Dubbed
"The King of Broadway," Jolson was America's most famous
and highly paid entertainer of the 1920s.

B. G. De Sylva
Louis Silvers, 1921

Arr. G. Weiser

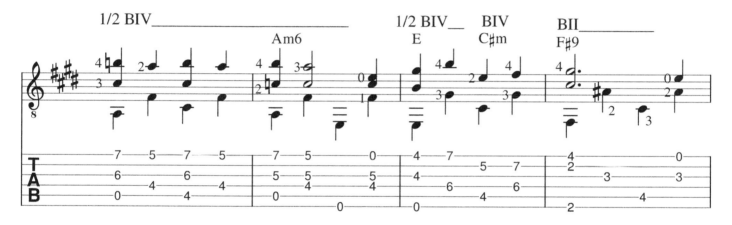

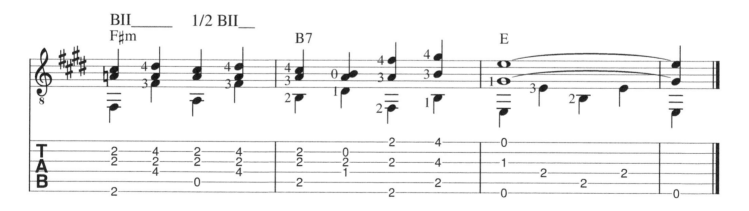

15

Bill Bailey, Won't You Please Come Home?

Hughie Cannon was a pianist at Conrad Deidrich's Saloon in Jackson, Michigan, where Willard "Bill" Bailey was a regular customer. Cannon wrote this Dixieland standard about Bailey's wife Sarah after she locked out Bill one night for staying too late at the bar.

Hughie Cannon, 1902

Arr. G. Weiser

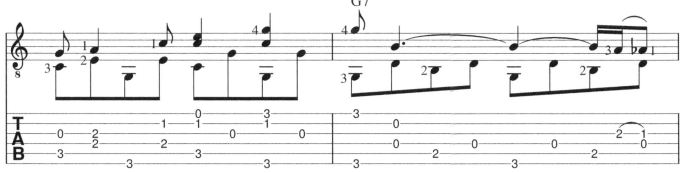

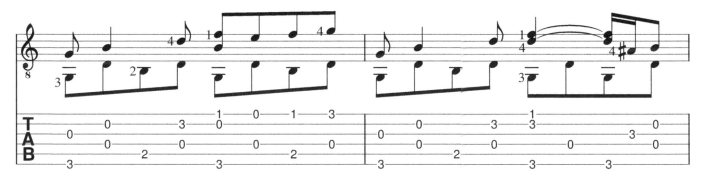

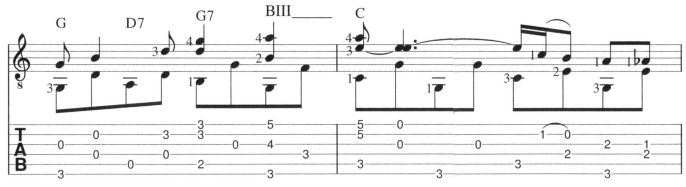

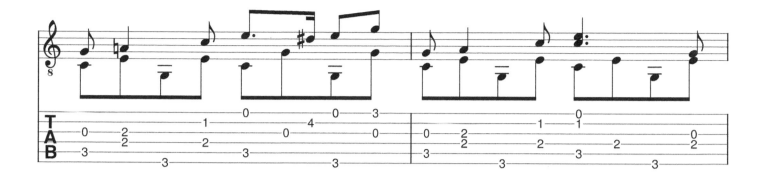

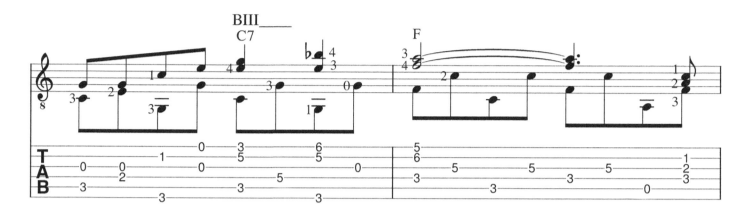

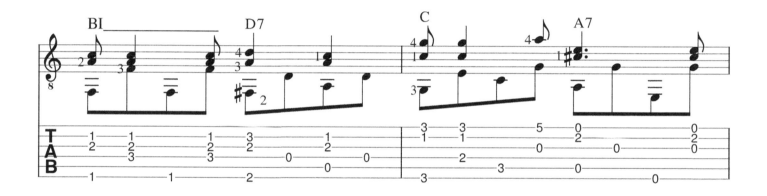

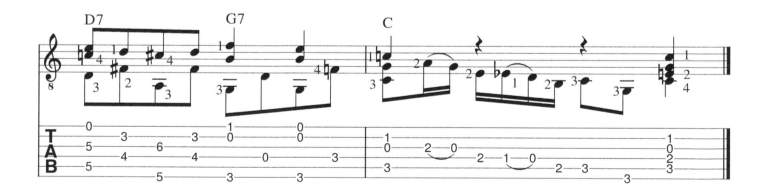

17

California, Here I Come

Al Jolson
Bud De Sylva
Joseph Meyer, 1921

This exuberant salute to the Golden State debuted
in the 1921 musical *Bombo*, starring Al Jolson.

Arr. G. Weiser

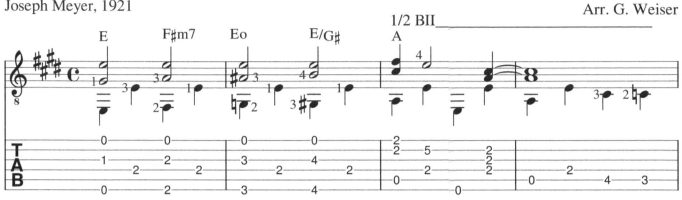

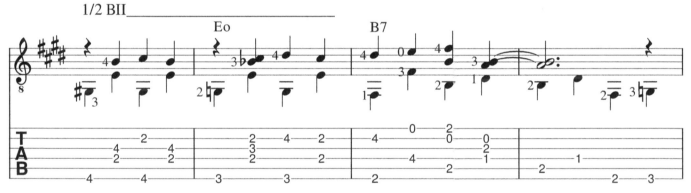

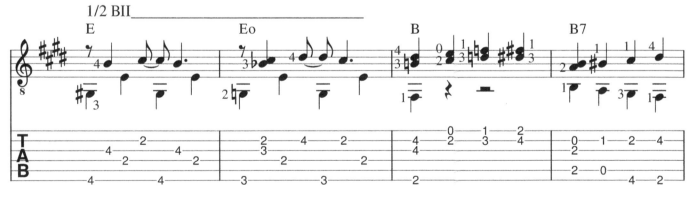

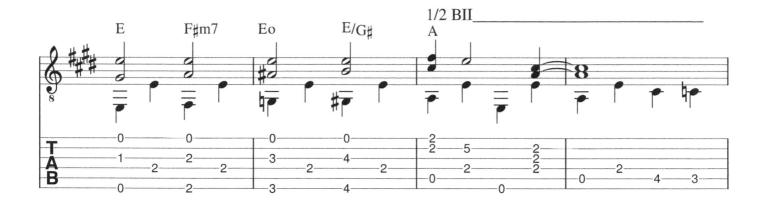

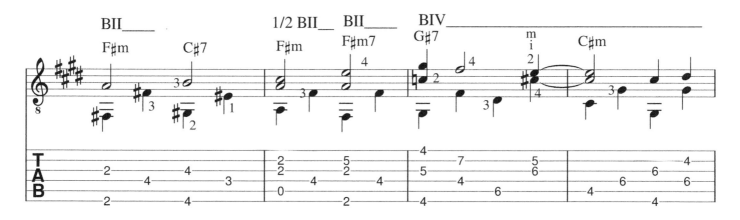

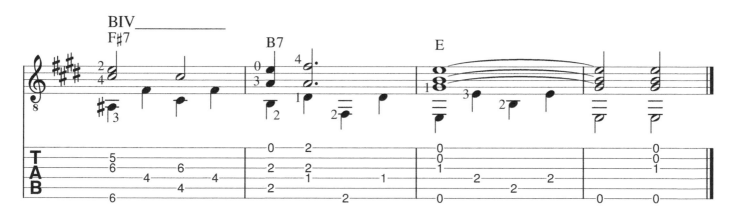

19

Carolina In The Morning

This song debuted in the risque revue *The Passing Show of 1922*. Together and separately,
Gus Kahn and Walter Donaldson wrote many of Tin Pan Alley's greatest hits.

Gus Kahn
Walter Donaldson, 1922

Arr. G. Weiser

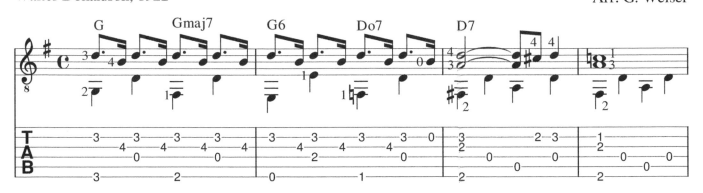

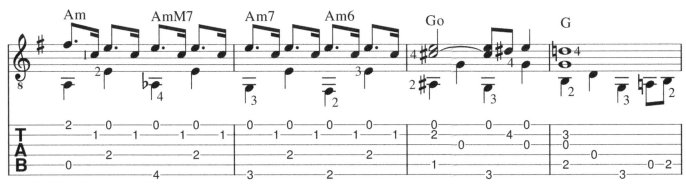

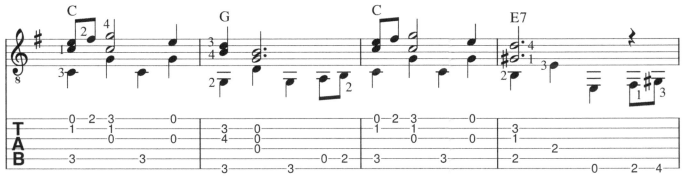

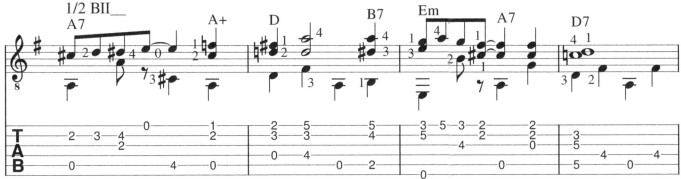

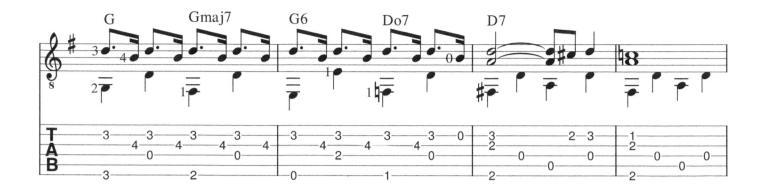

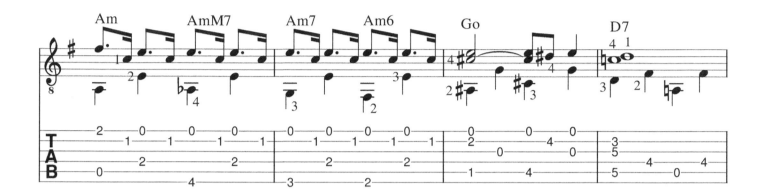

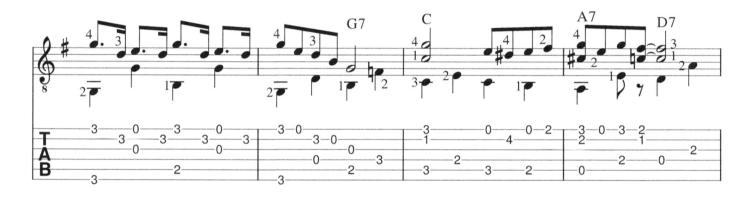

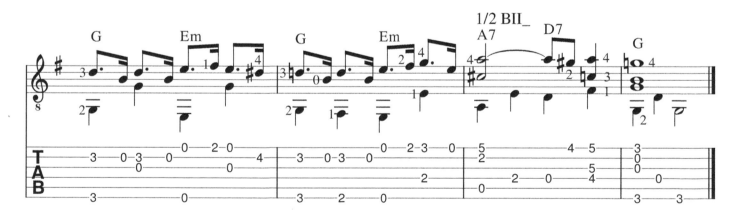

Charleston

Cecil Mack (Richard Cecil McPherson) and stride piano pioneer James P. Johnson wrote this hit
to accompany the Charleston dance in the black musical *Runnin' Wild*.

Cecil Mack
Jimmy Johnson, 1923

Arr. G. Weiser

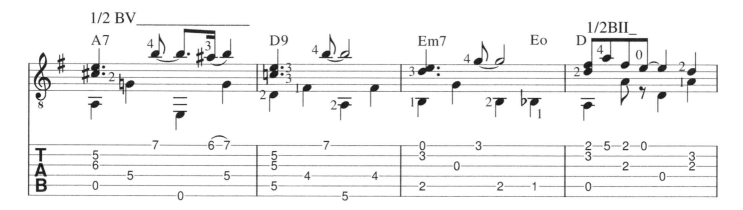

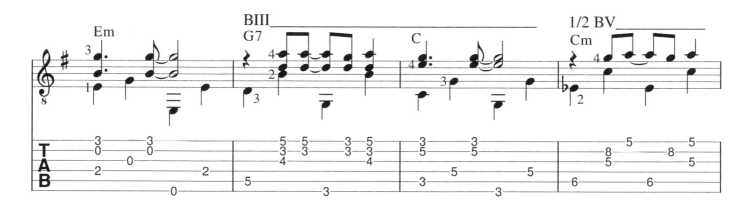

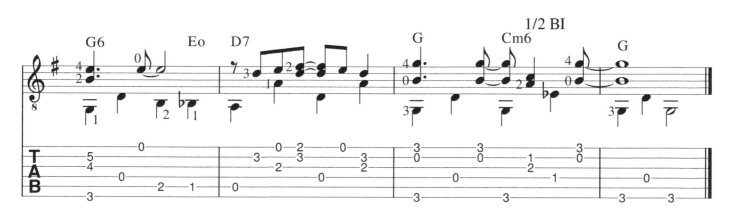

Chicago (That Todd'lin Town)

During the "sinful, ginful" 1920s, the bands of Louis Armstrong, Jimmy Noone, King Oliver,
and others spearheaded the evolution of jazz in the large dance halls along State Street
on Chicago's South Side. The Toddle was a slow, sensual dance like the Shimmy.

Fred Fisher, 1922

Arr. G. Weiser

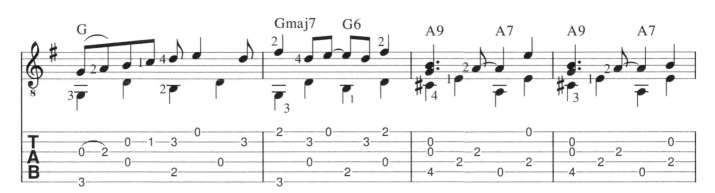

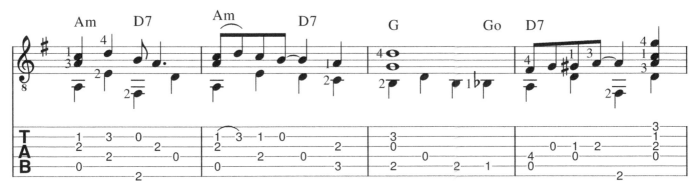

24

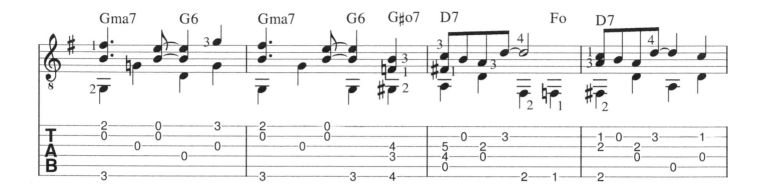

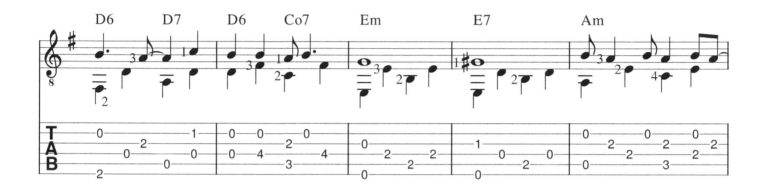

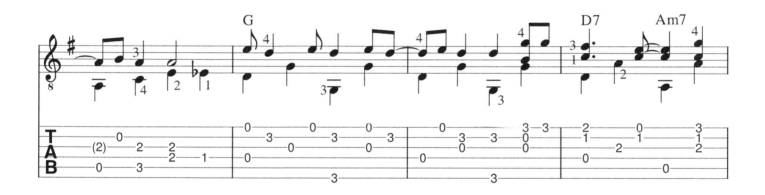

Chinatown, My Chinatown

Written in 1906, this catchy song was featured in the 1910 musical
Up and Down Broadway but was not a national hit until 1915.

William Jerome
Jean Schwartz, 1906

Arr. G. Weiser

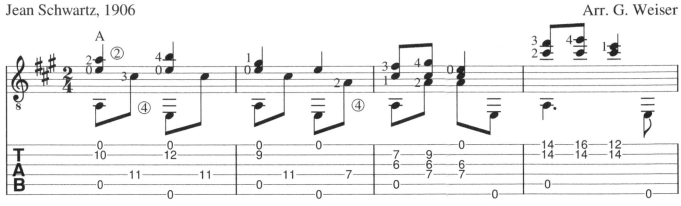

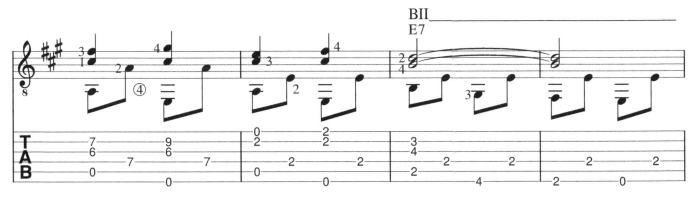

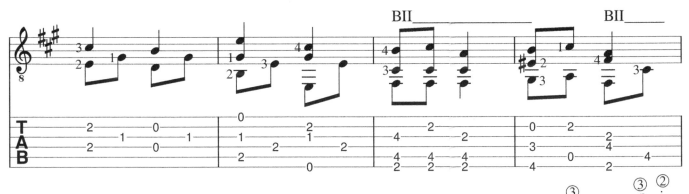

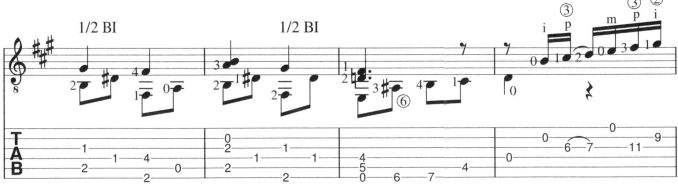

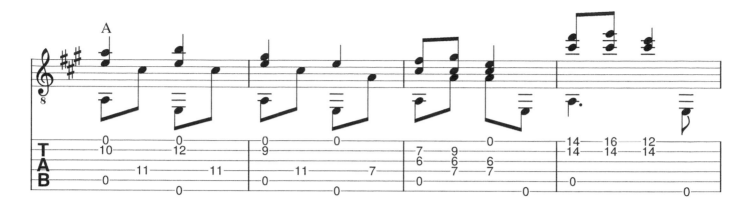

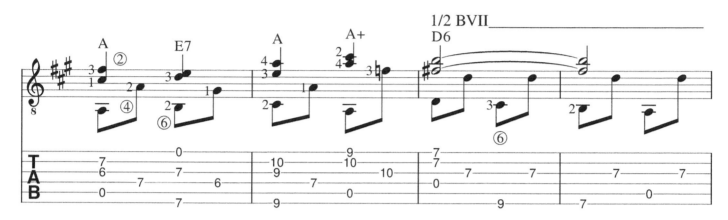

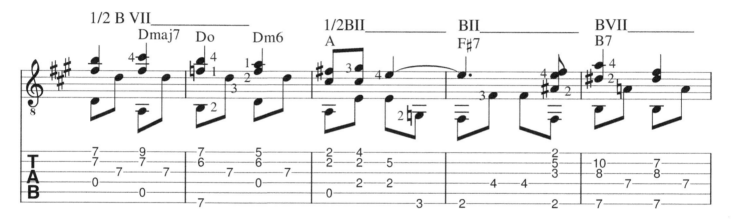

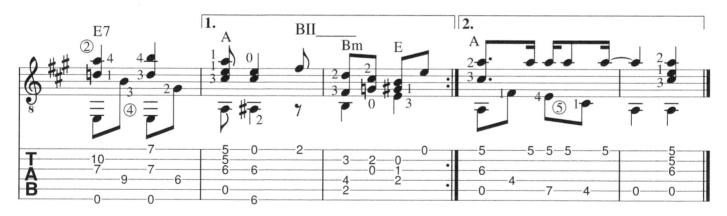

27

I'll See You In My Dreams

Long a guitarists' favorite, this 1925 #1 hit has been covered by
Django Reinhardt, Merle Travis, and Chet Atkins among others.

Gus Kahn
Isham Jones, 1924

Arr. G. Weiser

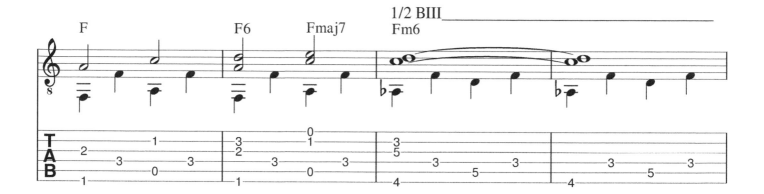

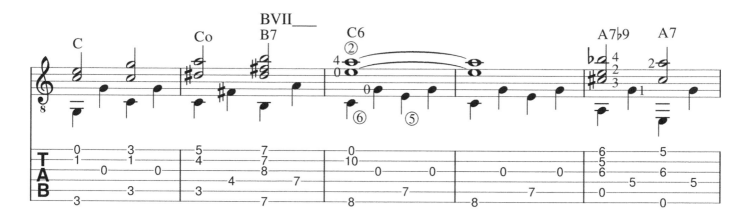

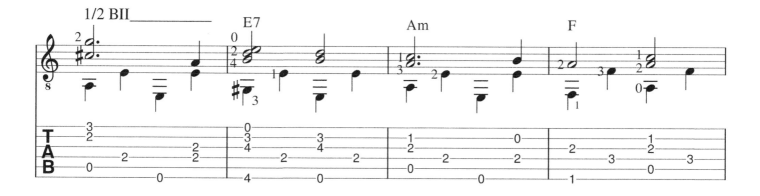

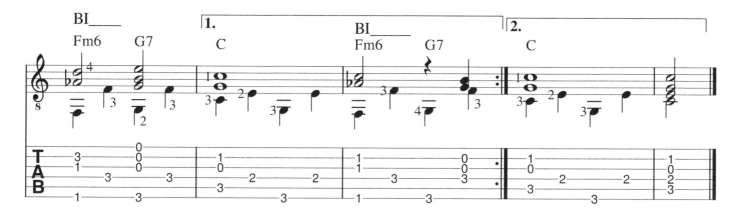

Indiana

Popularly known as *Back Home Again In Indiana*, this cheery uptempo song became a jazz standard.
This arrangement is for Centerstream's publisher, Ron Middlebrook,
whose family hails from the Hoosier State.

Ballard MacDonald
James F. Hanley, 1917

Arr. G. Weiser

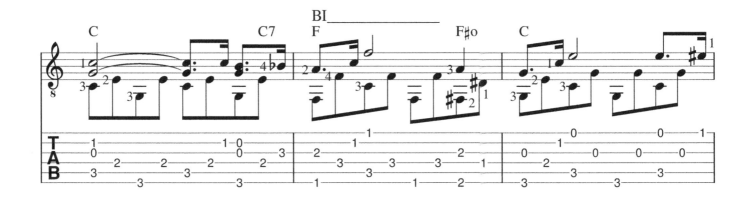

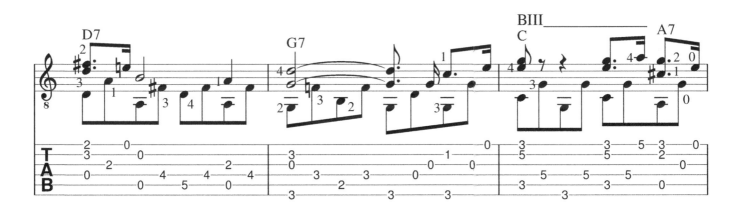

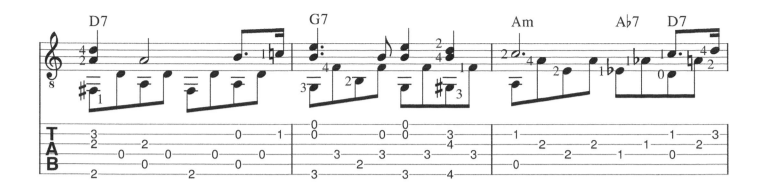

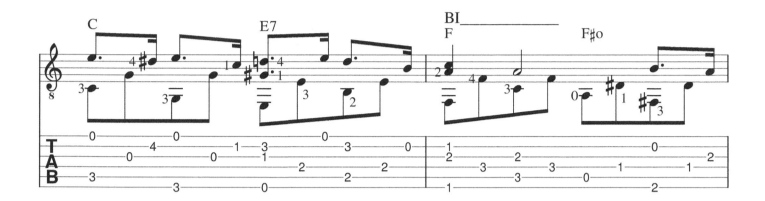

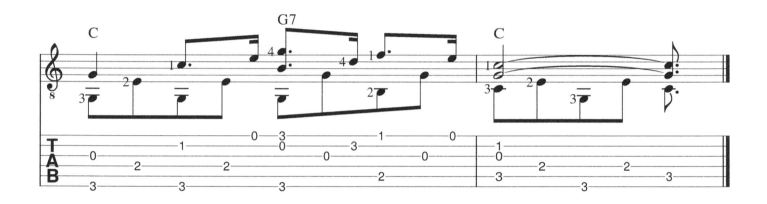

It Had To Be You

When Isham Jones' wife gave him a new piano for his 30th birthday, the tunesmith
composed four songs in an hour, including this one and *I'll See You in My Dreams*.
Betty Hutton sings it in the 1944 film *Incendiary Blonde*.

Gus Kahn

Isham Jones, 1924

Arr. G. Weiser

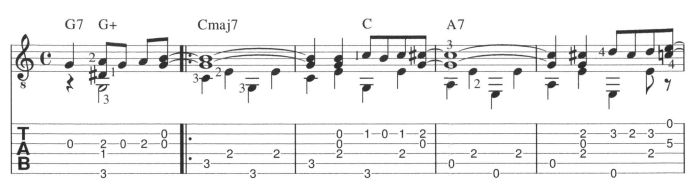

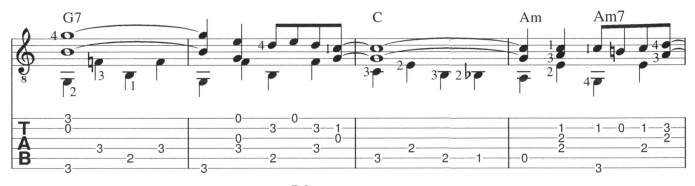

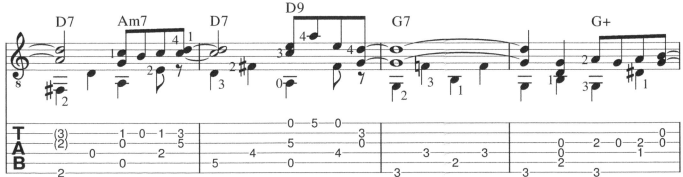

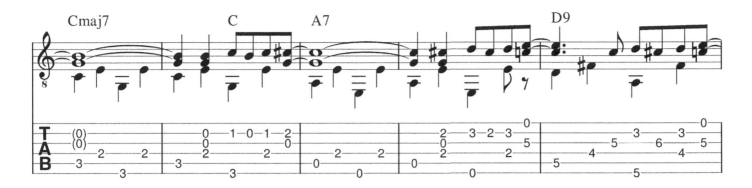

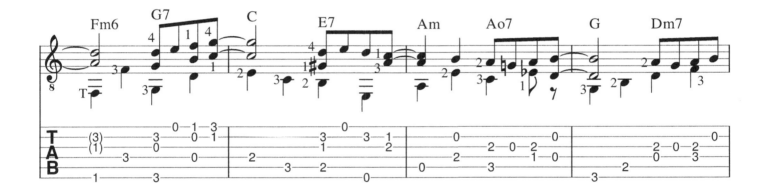

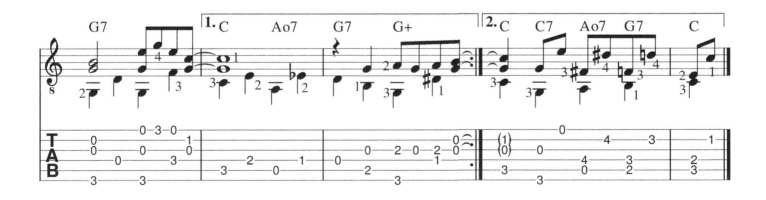

Limehouse Blues

Before WWI, London's Limehouse district was the city's Chinatown. This song is
from the 1921 revue *A to Z* and is usually heard in uptempo double-time versions.
This arrangement is closer to the original sheet music.

Douglas Furber
Philip Braham, 1921

Arr. G. Weiser

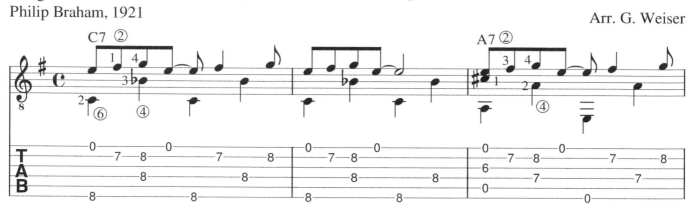

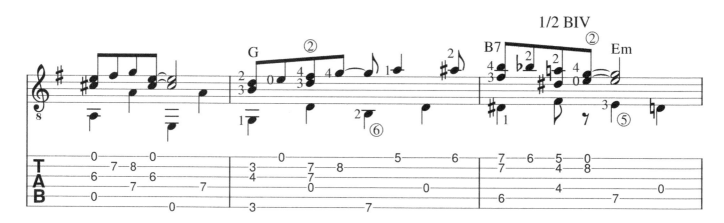

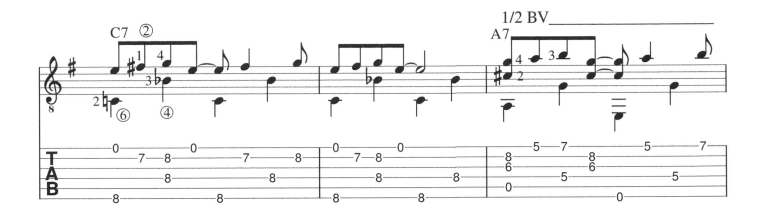

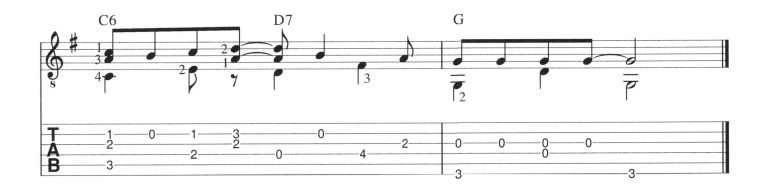

Lovesick Blues

This Tin Pan Alley tune was Hank Williams' first country chart #1
in 1949. It became his signature song and show closer.
I've arranged the original version here.

Irving Mills
Cliff Friend, 1922

Arr. G. Weiser

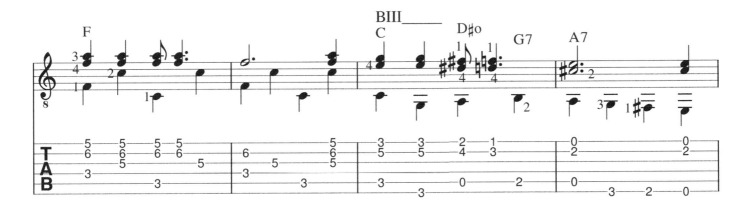

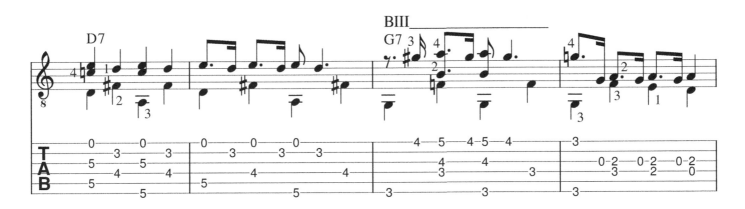

2

37

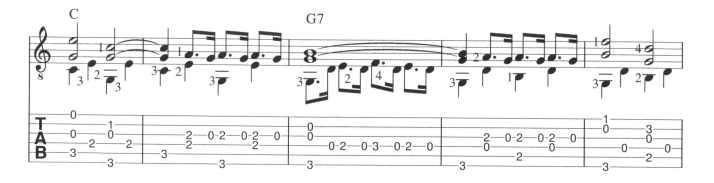

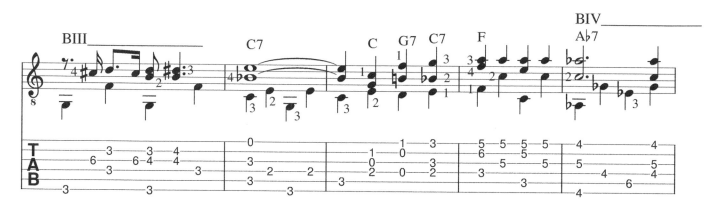

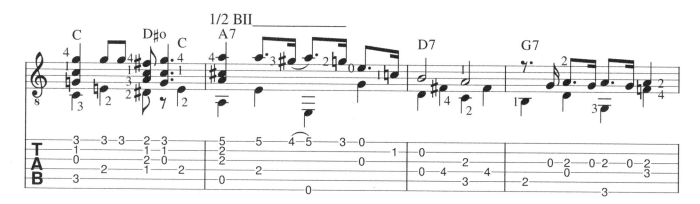

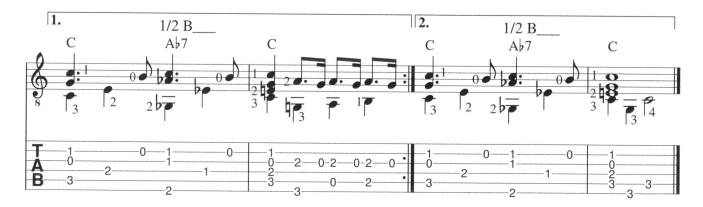

Meet Me In St. Louis, Louis

The 1904 Louisiana Purchase Exposition in St. Louis marked the centenary of the
Louis and Clark Expedition. This song was written to promote
the world's fair and became an instant hit.

Andrew B. Sterling
Kerry Mills, 1904

Arr. G. Weiser

The Man I Love

Music writer David Ewen considers this dreamy ballad the finest Tin Pan Alley song of them all.

George and Ira Gershwin, 1924

Arr. G. Weiser

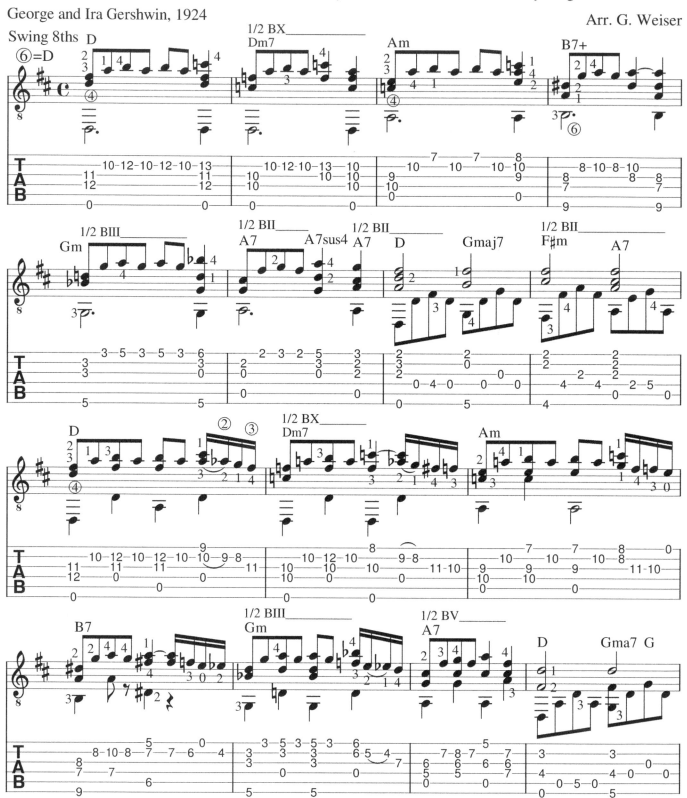

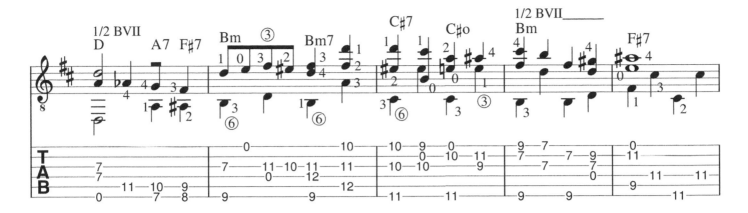

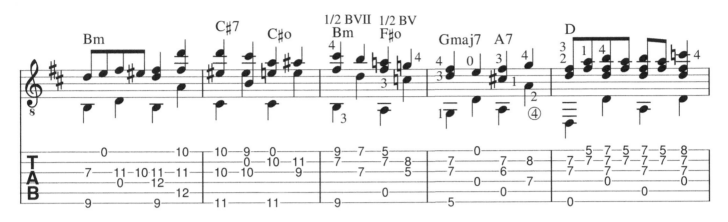

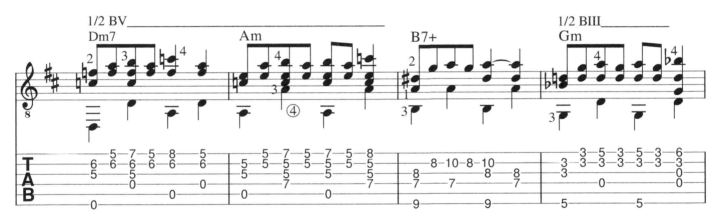

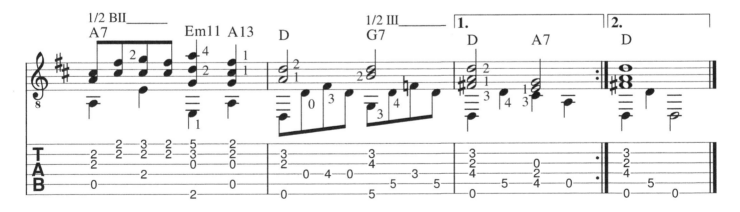

41

Nobody Knows You When You're Down and Out

This blues classic about fair-weather friends became popular in 1929 when Bessie Smith recorded it.
Eric Clapton and Duane Allman included it on Clapton's landmark 1970 album *Layla*.

Jimmy Cox, 1923

Arr. G. Weiser

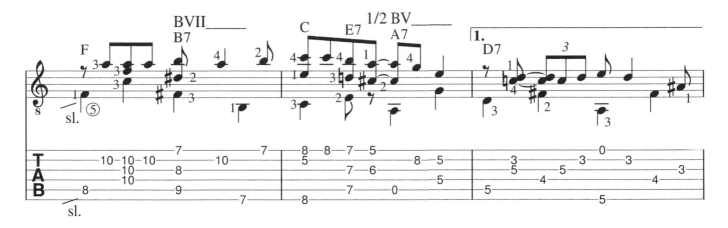

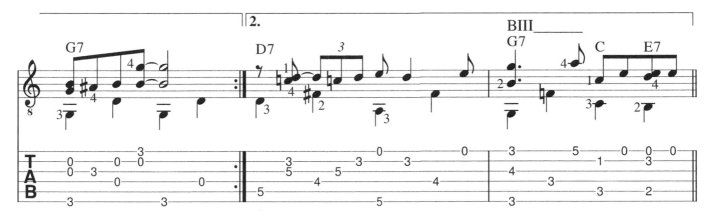

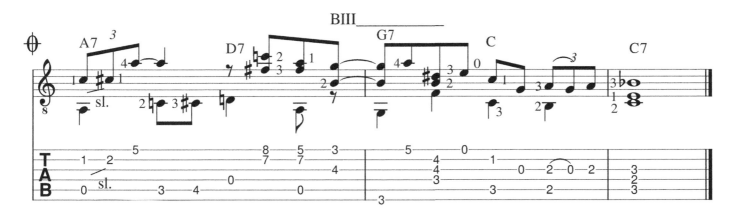

My Melancholy Baby

Ernie Burnett, the composer, was wounded in WWI and completely lost his memory along with his
identifying dog tags. When a pianist visited the hospital and played
this song, Burnett instantly regained total recall.

George A. Norton
Ernie Burnett, 1912

Arr. G. Weiser

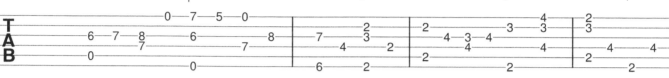

Oh, You Beautiful Doll

Ragtime rhythms abound in this 1911 hit, which has been
recorded hundreds of times and featured in several films.

Seymour Brown
Nat D. Ayer, 1911

Arr. G. Weiser

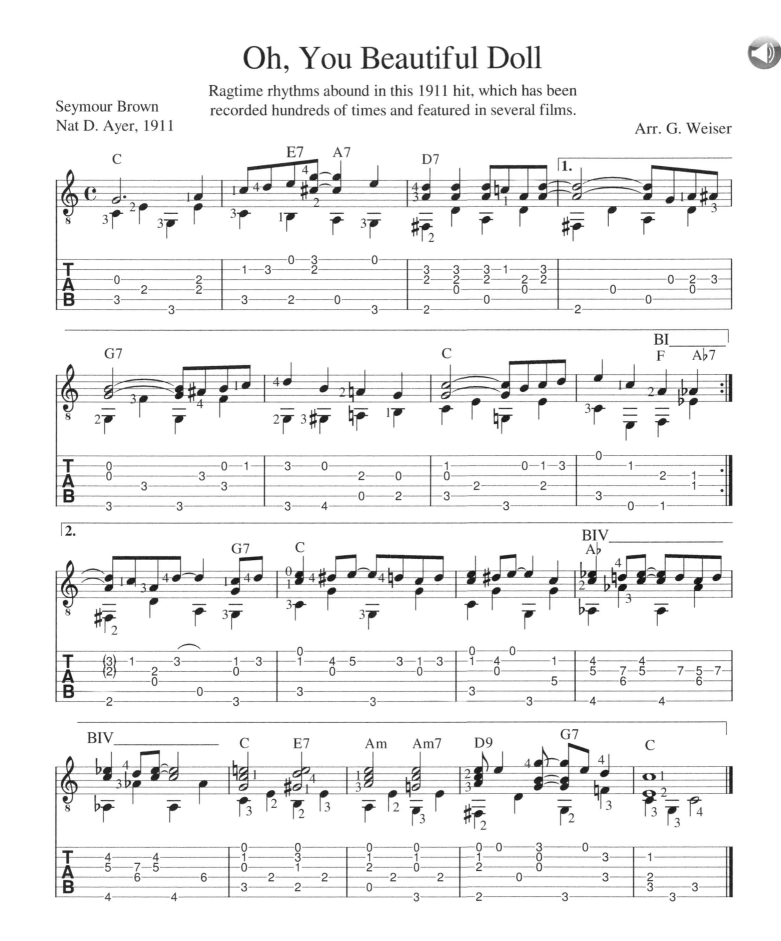

Somebody Stole My Gal

This popular song was recorded by many artists during the Chicago Jazz and Swing eras.

Leo Wood, 1918

Arr. G. Weiser

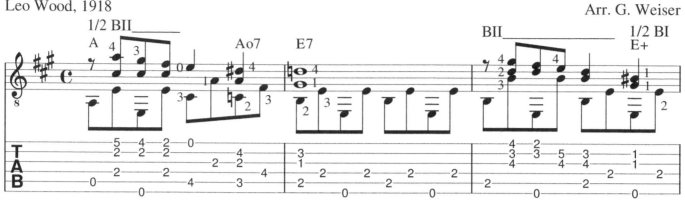

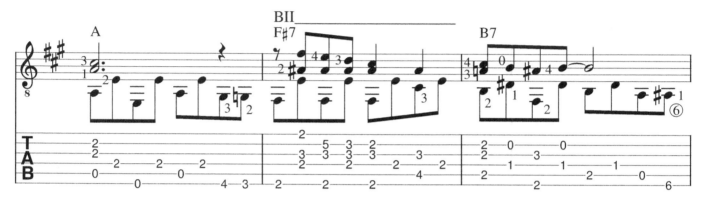

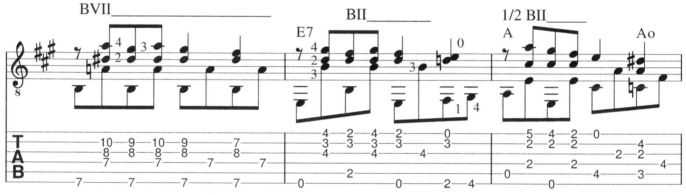

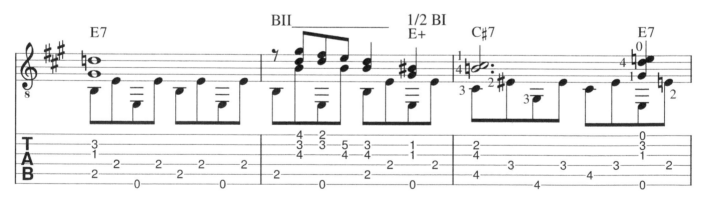

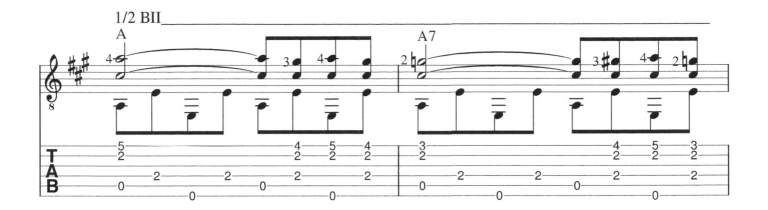

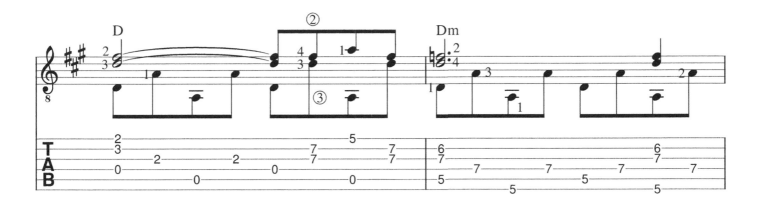

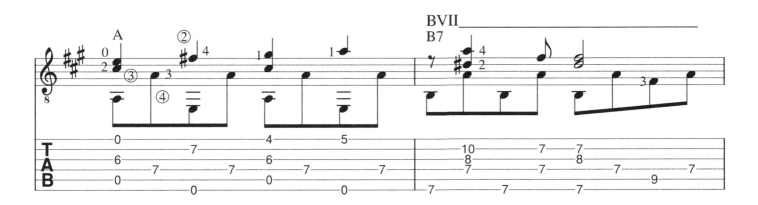

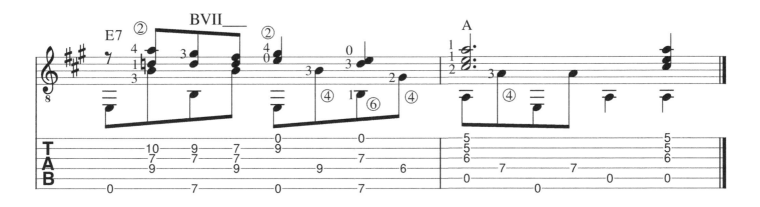

Pretty Baby

Originally penned by New Orleans pianist Tony Jackson about his male lover,
tunesmiths Gus Kahn and Ebert Van Alstyne rewrote the verse
and the lyrics for the revue *A World of Pleasure.*

Gus Kahn
Tony Jackson
Ebert Van Alstyne, 1916

Arr. G. Weiser

St. Louis Blues

This celebrated song is one of the earliest published 12-bar blues, and has been called "the jazzman's *Hamlet.*" According to John Lomax, Leadbelly sung it years before W. C. Handy claimed authorship.

W. C. Handy, 1914

Arr. G. Weiser

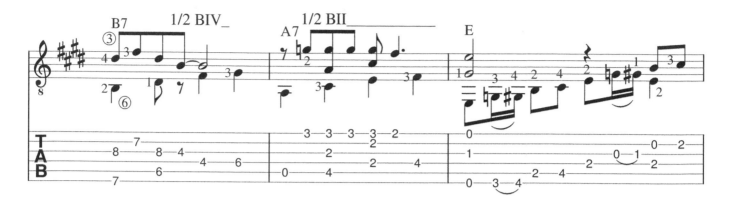

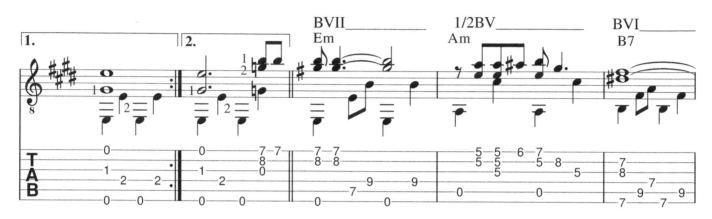

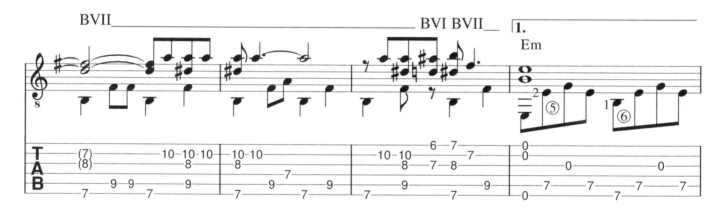

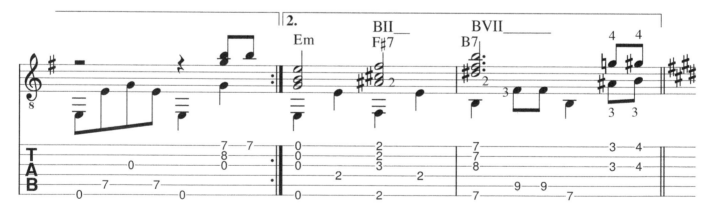

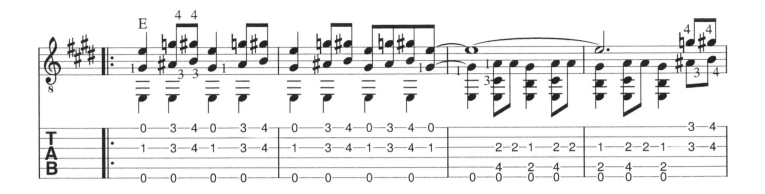

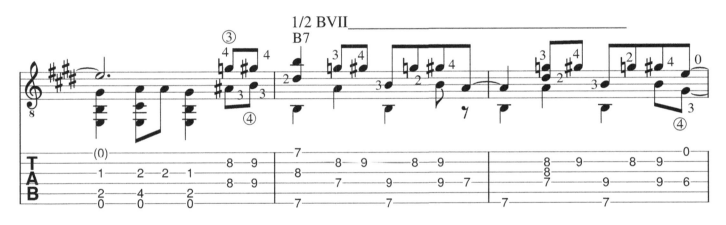

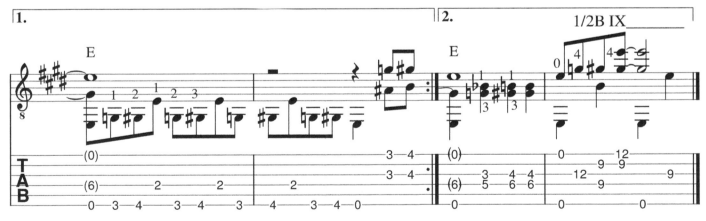

Take Me Out To The Ball Game

Although this song became the unofficial anthem of baseball, neither the composer nor the lyricist had ever been to a ballgame prior to writing it.

Jack Norworth
Albert Von Tilzer, 1908

Arr. G. Weiser

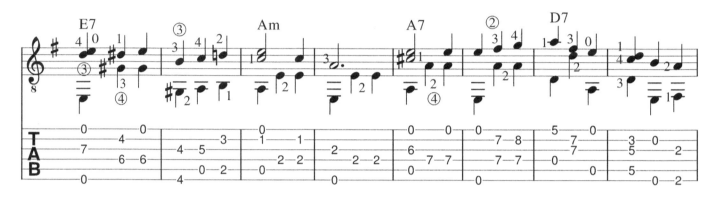

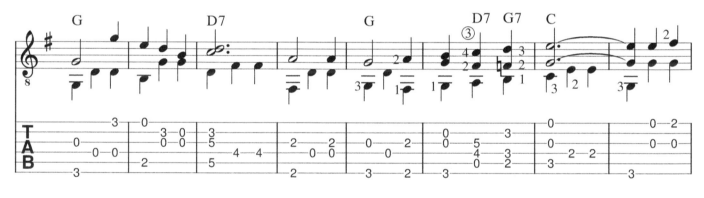

When Irish Eyes Are Smiling

Chauncy Olcott
Geo. Graff Jr.
Earnest R. Ball, 1912

This famous song was featured in the 1913 musical *The Isle O' Dreams.* Groucho Marx once got thrown out of Parliament after he stood and sang it in the visitors' gallery.

Arr. G. Weiser

Tea for Two

Introduced in the 1925 musical *No, No, Nanette*, the title quotes an 18th century London street hawkers' cry advertising a pot of tea for the bargain price of two pence. I play this with a swing feel.

Irving Caesar
Vincent Youmans, 1924

Arr. G. Weiser

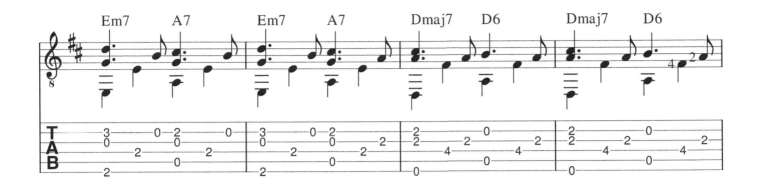

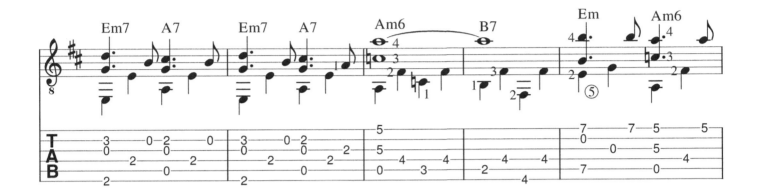

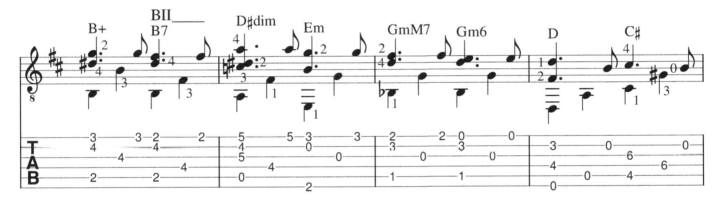

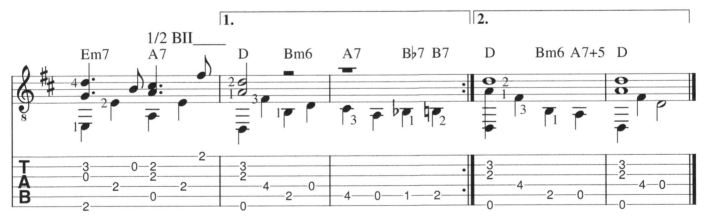

Way Down Yonder in New Orleans

Introduced in the Broadway revue *Spice of 1922,* this bouncy tune became a
Chicago jazz favorite, with versions recorded by Louis Armstrong,
Bix Beiderbecke, Jimmie Noone, and Sidney Bechet.

Turner Layton

Henry Creamer, 1922

Arr. G. Weiser

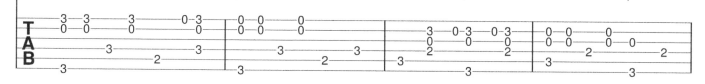

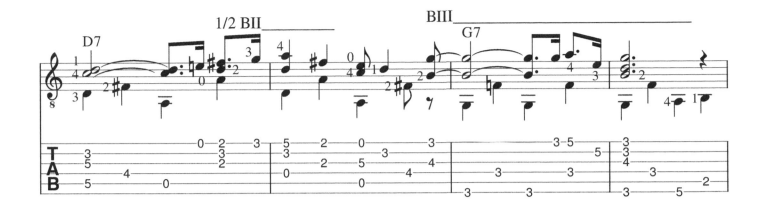

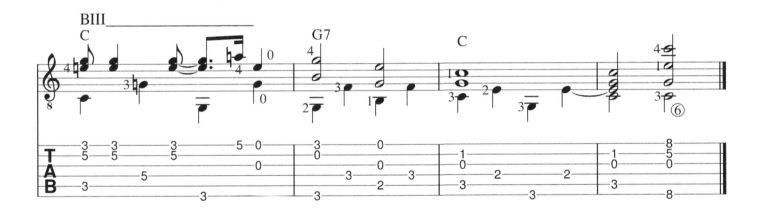

Whispering

Considered the song that opened the Jazz Age, this was the first major hit for Paul Whiteman and His Orchestra, the leading "sweet" jazz band (as opposed to the "hot" black bands) of the era.

Malvin & John Schonberger, 1920

Arr. G. Weiser

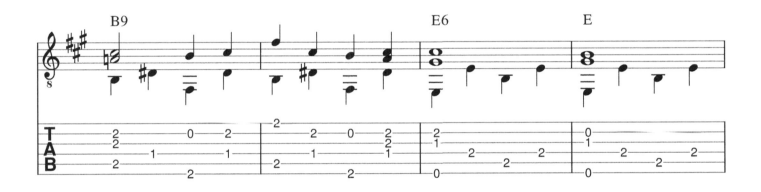

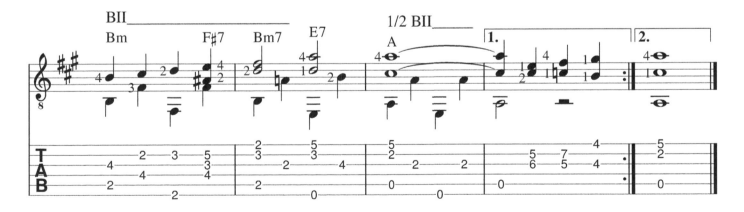

The Yankee Doodle Boy

This catchy hit was featured in George M. Cohan's first full-length musical, *Little Johnny Jones*.
You can hear James Cagney sing it in the 1942 film *Yankee Doodle Dandy*.

George M. Cohan, 1904

Arr. G. Weiser

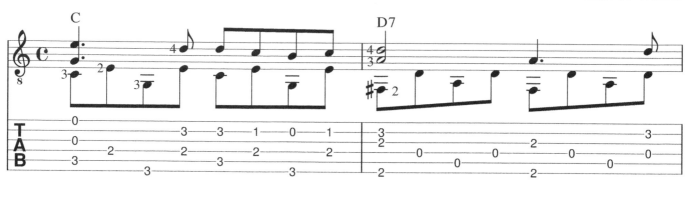

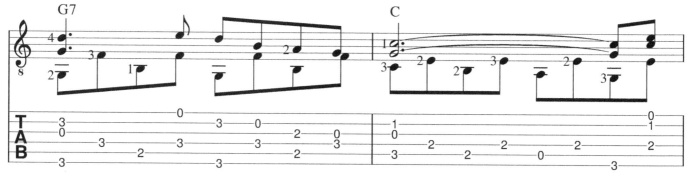

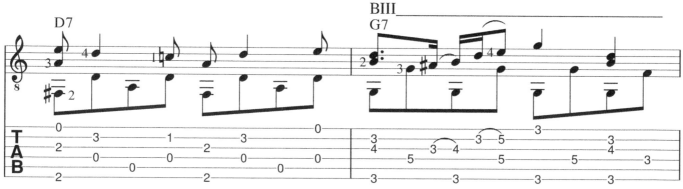

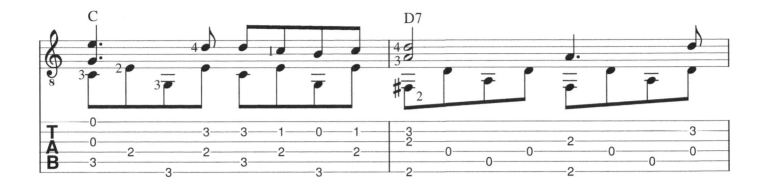

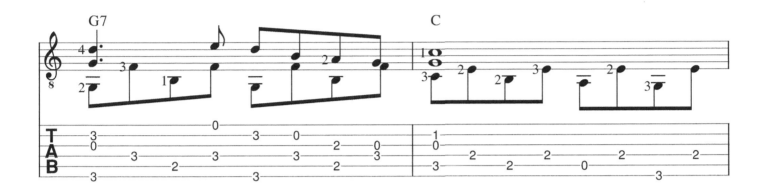

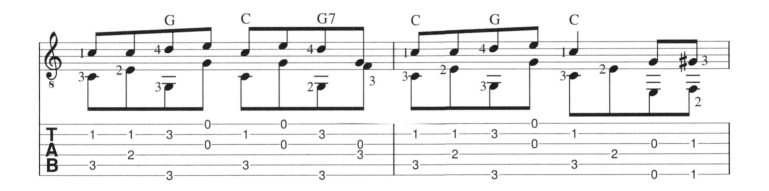

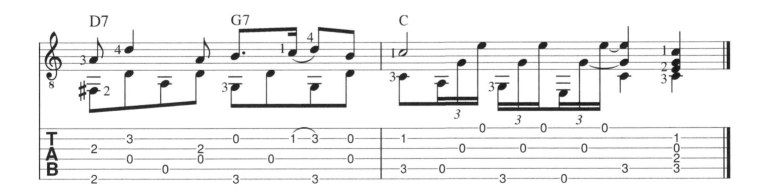

61

You're A Grand Old Flag

Originally entitled "You're A Grand Old Rag," this debuted in George M. Cohan's musical comedy *George Washington Jr.* It was the first song from a Broadway show to sell a million copies in sheet music.

Geo. M. Cohan, 1906

Arr. G. Weiser

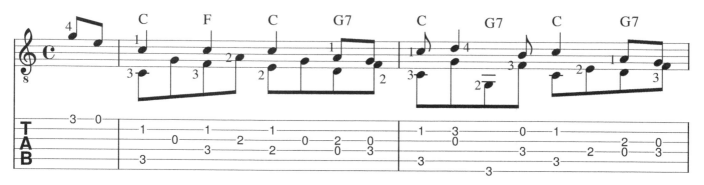

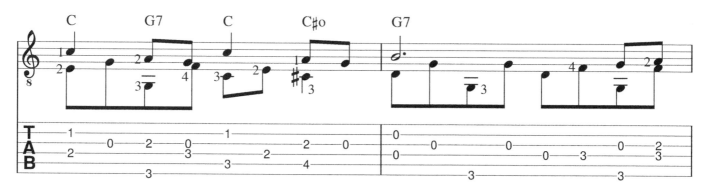

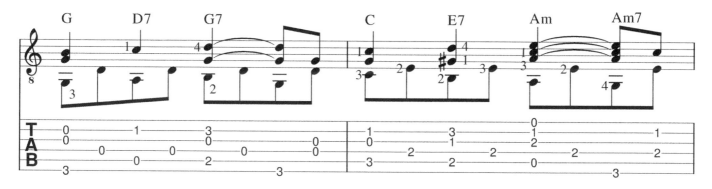

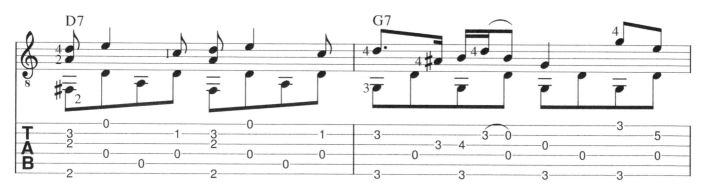

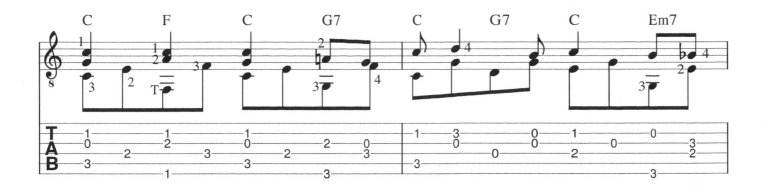

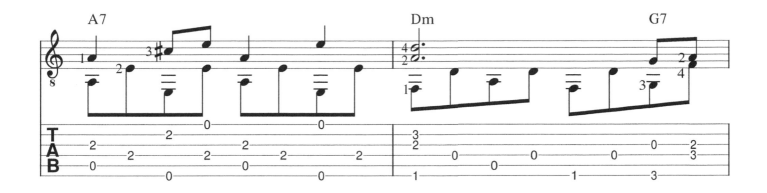

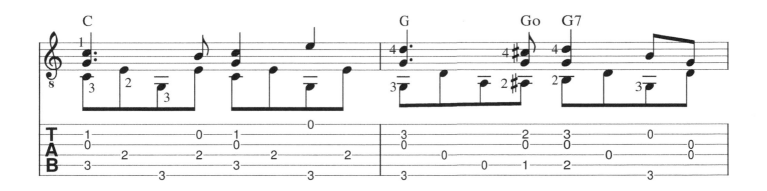

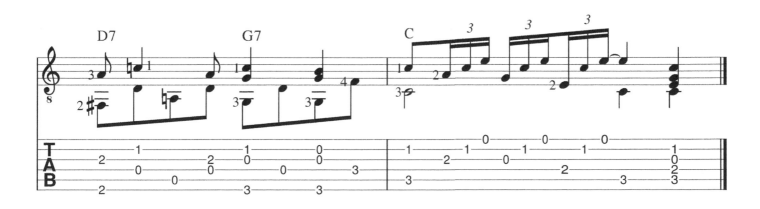

More Great Guitar Books from Centerstream...

SCALES & MODES IN THE BEGINNING
by Ron Middlebrook

The most comprehensive and complete scale book written especially for the guitar. Chapers include: Fretboard Visualization • Scale Terminology • Scales and Modes • and a Scale to Chord Guide.
00000010...$11.95

CELTIC CITTERN
by Doc Rossi

Although the cittern has a history spanning 500 years and several countries, like its cousin the Irish bouzouki, it is a relative newcomer to contemporary traditional music. Doc Rossi, a wellknown citternist in both traditional and early music, has created this book for intermediate to advanced players who want to improve their technique, develop ideas and learn new repertoire. Guitarists can play all of the tunes in this book on the guitar by tuning C F C G C F, low to high, and putting a capo at the second fret. The lowest line in the tablature then corresponds to the fifth string. The CD features all the tunes played at a medium tempo.
00001460 Book/CD Pack...$19.99

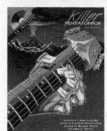

KILLER PENTATONICS FOR GUITAR
by Dave Celentano

Covers innovative and diverse ways of playing pentatonic scales in blues, rock and heavy metal. The licks and ideas in this book will give you a fresh approach to playing the pentatonic scale, hopefully inspiring you to reach for higher levels in your playing. The 37-minute companion CD features recorded examples.

00000285 Book/CD Pack..$19.95

MELODY CHORDS FOR GUITAR
by Allan Holdsworth

Influential fusion player Allan Holdsworth provides guitarists with a simplified method of learning chords, in diagram form, for playing accompaniments and for playing popular melodies in "chord-solo" style. Covers: major, minor, altered, dominant and diminished scale notes in chord form, with lots of helpful reference tables and diagrams.

00000222...$24.95

PAINLESS ARRANGING FOR OLD-TIME COUNTRY GUITAR
by Joe Weidlich This book will help readers recognize and remember commonly used note patterns and sequences in fiddle tunes and string band music, to make creating interesting variations easier. Author Joe Weidlich analyzes four traditional favorites – including "The Wreck of the Old '97" – showing how guitarists can substitute notes and patterns, painlessly!
00001353 ....$14.99

COMPLETE RHYTHM GUITAR GUIDE FOR BLUES BANDS
by Larry McCabe

This info-filled book/CD will take you out of your rhythm-playing rut and teach you to play confidently in any blues style! You'll learn: intros, endings and turnarounds; modern theory for reharmonizing chord progressions; jazz and eight-bar progressions; and much more. The book includes 100 musical examples, 16 theory workshops, a discography and bibliography, and the CD has 51 tracks.
00000333 Book/CD Pack...$24.95

GUITAR CHORDS PLUS
by Ron Middlebrook

A comprehensive study of normal and extended chords, tuning, keys, transposing, capo use, and more. Includes over 500 helpful photos and diagrams, a key to guitar symbols, and a glossary of guitar terms.
00000011..$11.95

THE CHORD SCALE GUIDE
by Greg Cooper

The Chord Scale Guide will open up new voicings for chords and heighten your awareness of linear harmonization. This will benefit jazz ensemble players, rock guitarists and songwriters looking to create new and unique original music, and understand the harmony behind chords.
00000324..$15.95

 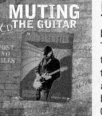

IRISH YOU A MERRY CHRISTMAS
by Doug Esmond

This book includes Christmas melodies as well as lesserknown tunes from Scotland paired with seasonal titles. All the songs can be played solo or with other instruments. A CD is included with recordings of the author playing using both steel and nylon string guitars.
00001360 Book/CD Pack...$15.99

MUTING THE GUITAR
by David Brewster

This book/CD pack teaches guitarists how to effectively mute anything! Author David Brewster covers three types of muting in detail: frethand, pickhand, and both hands. He provides 65 examples in the book, and 70 tracks on the accompanying CD.
00001199 Book/CD Pack...$19.99

P.O. Box 17878 - Anaheim Hills, CA 92817
(714) 779-9390   www.centerstream-usa.com